D1070815

To the memory of our parents
To the benefit of Hungary
To the glory of God

László Mészáros *Natural Treasures of*

HUNGARY

Balaton

Danube

Tisza

Mountains

Puszta

OFFICINA '96 KIADÓ

INTRODUCTION

I greet the reader! And with frank respect, I greet the author, the former student of Sárospatak, the lover of Zemplén county, and the artist with his penchant for the most Hungarian of our rivers, the Tisza, which as we all know, has undergone many trials and tribulations recently. I pay my respects to this photographer, this master of the camera, who has reached the zenith of his twenty year long career, just as I greet this passionate, thought provoking man who understands nature so deeply. László Mészáros here gives a superb review of Hungary's natural treasures. He has examined things that others in Hungary tend to overlook. But they represent an irreplacable natural treasure, with which Hungary can justly add to Europe's heritage. This millenium selection is a wise and spectacular one. It is wise, because it presents some of the most characteristic natural landscapes in Hungary, as well as some of those endangered animals and plants that inhabit them. And it is spectacular in the true sense of the word, because his photos are more than simply the superb products of end of the century technology. This book is a sensitve and thoughtful artist's tribute to the environment he lives in. And it is a warning to us all: we have much to lose, and much is at stake. Just how long we can enjoy Hungary's woods and rivers, plains and caves, depends very much on us all. Our actions decide for just how much longer we can enjoy the sound of our larks, the phenomeonon of cranes in the sky, the play of grey herons by the water, the sight of kingfishers and spotted redshanks, not to mention the appearance of rare orchids in our forests and marshlands. How much longer can we boast that the meadow viper only lives in Hungary, or that the acquatic warbler nests here? László Mészáros' picture of Hungary is uplifting, reassuring and thought provoking. To the mind, eye, and soul alike. He deserves to be thanked for it. By us all. I'd like to wish all our readers the most enjoyable country expeditions, as they follow in László Mészáros' footsteps.

JÁNOS TARDY

Deputy Secretary of State, Head of Authority for Nature Conservation, Ministry of Environment

Lake Balaton

These houses in the village of Salföld are typical of the architecture of the Balaton Uplands.

In geological antiquity, the Lake Balaton region was covered by a shallow sea. Later, the "Pannonian sea" became an internal lake, with its water losing its salinity. The protuberant ridges formed five separate partial basins, which, some twenty to twenty-five thousand years ago, merged into one, yielding today's lake-basin. In rainy periods, the water surface could cover an area twice as large as it is today. In the early 19th century, the water level was still four to five metres higher than now. 1863 witnessed the construction of the Siófok sluice, allowing the water level of the lake to be kept lower. After 1945, the slogan of "Let Lake Balaton belong to everyone" caused much damage. A campaign to divide the region into a host of mini-plots resulted in the shores being covered with countless inferior buildings and weekend cottages; the shores of Lake Balaton were paved with concrete nearly all the way round; there was a considerable dwindling of the ancient reed-grass vegetation and a gradual silting up of the Keszthely bay. The reed began to die, and the carved-up reedy areas were no longer able to cope with what had earlier been such an important function. The massive dying of fish and the algal invasion, sent a warning signal goading the experts to take effective action. With the focus now on environmental protection regulations, the "Small Balaton" was given back its role as a filter; and the establishment of the Balaton Uplands National Park allowed the criteria of nature conservation to be given their due. By the end of the millennium, the water quality of the lake had visibly improved, with changes to be discerned in all areas – changes giving hope that one of our greatest natural treasures, lake Balaton, may be restored to its former glory.

Lake Balaton is one of the largest lakes in Central Europe, a continuing summer destination for the inhabitants of both Hungary and numerous European countries, a tourist magnet. Some visit it because of the charming scenery, while others are attracted by the bustling life, the disco atmosphere of summer nights; but there are those, too, who come here in search of tranquillity and rest. Devotees of fish and fishing swear by its excellent opportunities; but Lake Balaton is a paradise for lovers of water, sailing, and surfing as well. People in search of a cure come here because of the medicinal waters of Balatonfüred or Hévíz. And a sizeable portion of excursionists are curious to see the castles and sights of the Balaton Uplands. And, certainly, the Balaton wines, the hospitable atmosphere of the wine-cellars, must also be included among the ingredients of that magic appeal.

But what is it that really makes the lake so appealing, unique and inimitable for so many people? It owes its appeal to the combination of the sunshine, the water, and the scenery. The sunshine is Mediterranean, the water is silken and soft. The time to really appreciate the beauty of the landscape is from autumn to spring, once the droves of tourists have cleared out. The glacial formations of Lake Balaton during the winter are unique. The enormous water surface takes a long time to develop a more solid encrustation of ice. The thick frozen areas, then, crack into huge crevasses amidst noises reminiscent of cannon-shots.

Spring comes very early to the Lake Balaton district: as early as February, you see flocks – numbering thousands – of wild geese, wild ducks and coots awaiting the arrival of spring on the water full of ice-floes. In the protected valleys of the Balaton Uplands, the winter aconite and snowdrops open their petals; on the hillsides, the old almond trees – each with a history of its own – begin to blossom already in March; and, within a short time, all the trees and bushes burst into bloom in the meadows, the vineyards and in the gardens too. It is in spring that the neighbourhood of Lake Balaton is most beautiful – that is the season that crowns the beauty of the Balaton Uplands.

The Inner Lake at Tihany

So there is a wealth of ingredients to the appeal of Lake Balaton; but there is an even greater wealth of natural values. The Small Balaton has been a nature protection area since 1951. Conservationists around the world have always been aware of it; and the Ramsari Convention included it in the category of "Internationally important wild waters". It was in 1952 that Hungary's first landscape protection area was established in the pearl of Lake Balaton, the Tihany peninsula. The peninsula is home to many tropical plant and animal rarities. The district of remnant hills – each in the shape of a truncated cone – rising in the Tapolca Basin is unparalleled in Europe; France's district of volcanoes is the only region one could compare it to. Standing in the middle of the basin is the St. George Hill, encircled by a ring of volcanic cones facing each other. Located at the back of Lake Balaton and the wonderful hills is the Káli Basin, which, indeed, has until recently, been overshadowed by them; but its beauty was discovered by painters and artists already long long time ago. It is the geological assets that are the outstanding treasures of this basin; Hegyestű – of exotic beauty, with basalt columns, but divided in half because of quarrying – rises the highest from its plane. Its villages, of fairy-tale situation, the row of wine-cellars and the small-plot vineyards, and the tiny woods covering the hilltops merge in a picturesque view in the dawn mists that so often fill the basin. The preservation of the architectural values of the landscape and the fitting of new structures into the landscape are a project actively assisted by the local governments, in a manner, indeed, that could justly serve as an example throughout the country.

It was with the aim of cultivating the natural wealth of Lake Balaton and the Balaton Uplands that the Balaton Uplands National Park was established; in the Hegyestű, a geological education path and demonstration site was built; in Salföld, a nature protection visiting centre was set up; – everything is being done to preserve our natural treasures.

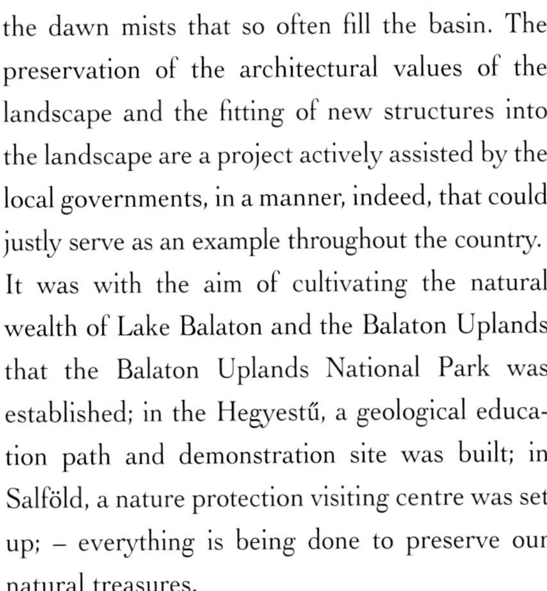

The Outer Lake, sitting in a volcanic crater at Tihany, is one of the finest in Hungary. Conservationists have restored it to its original condition. Seen from Kiserdő hill, the lake makes for a stunning spectacle. Note the varied forms of basalt tuff cliffs in the foreground.

The view from Badacsony offers an unmatchable panorama of the Szigetliget inlet, surely one of the finest sights in Hungary. This area is also known for the cultivation of grapes and fruit, which can be traced back to Roman times. All this natural splendour is supplemented by folk architecture, roadside shrines, as well as mansions and castle ruins.

Redshank Tringa totanus
This water wader, with its striking red legs, is hugely impressive when it takes to the air. Its appealing song can be heard from afar. Should you come too close to its nest, the redshank will cleverly distract you. It falls crying to the ground and seems to challenge you to follow it … away from its nest, naturally.

As the ice begins to melt, Balaton is suddenly abloom with flocks of ***coots.*** **Fulica atra**

Crambe tataria
At the turn of the century, this plant could only be found at Balatonkenese, but in recent years, it has established itself in other nearby localities. It is a traditional plant of the Eurasian steppeland, and can be found from Western Siberia to lower Austria.

Moorhen **Gallinula chloropus**
The moorhen is a peaceful bird and one of the jewels of the lake. It always keeps its tail held high, while swimming or on land, and characteristically nods its head with every movement. In the breeding season, moorhens can be seen leading their 8-10 nut sized, velvet black chicks, across the water.

Badacsony in early spring, with the almonds blossoming

Winter Aconite Eranthis hyemalis

The Hungarian folk name for this plant is "the winter burier", so named because it is one of the earliest plants to flower in Hungary, earlier even than snowdrops and wild hyacinths. It is a Mediterranean plant, and was probably introduced to this region by the Romans.

Yellow Day-lily

Hemerocallis lilio-asphodelus

The Belgian botanist Cladius, who frequently studied Hungarian fauna, found this plant near Németújvár at the end of the 16th century. From here, it spread to Western Europe, and starting in Austria, took its place in domestic gardens. Its cultivated varieties remain popular, but in its wild form, constitutes one of the rarities of the Balaton Uplands and Western Hungary. Its scientific name derives, appropriately, from the Greek meaning 'the beauty of the sun."

Sternbergia colchiciflora

The first botany professor of Buda university, Jakab Winterl, discovered this plant near Buda, and was christened by the distinguished scientist Pál Kitaibel. It only flowers at the end of September or early October after rain, which led to its role in folk culture as indication that time is ripe for autumn sowing.

A ravishing shot of lake Balaton taken at dawn.

***Siberian Iris* Iris sibirica**

Iris comes from the Greek word meaning rainbow, because this plant exhibits such a multitude of hues. The flowers of the Siberian iris tend to occupy the dark violet end of the spectrum. These plants can be found all over Eurasia, and grow across a wide swathe of territory in Hungary, in marshlands and also in many parts of the Balaton Uplands.

The stone sea at Szentbékkálla is one of the most renowned geological phenomena in Europe.
These huge stones, that have been preserved untouched, are arranged as if they were waves upon the sea.

On hot summer nights at the Tihany peninsula, you may be mistaken for thinking you are on the shores of the Mediterranean due to the endless chirruping cicadas **Tettigia orni**

Asphodel **Asphodelus albus**
The beauty of this plant's flower has inspired numerous poets and writers. The ancient Greeks believed that the souls of the dead inhabit meadows of Asphodelus. The plant occurs around the Mediterranean, but spread north to Hungary following the last ice age. This attractive rarity only occurs in western Hungary, and is best established in the Balaton Uplands.

Marsh Gentian **Gentiana pneumonanthe**
This species of the Gentian family tends to flourish at higher altitudes. With its large flowers, it is remarkably decorative. The Hungarian member of this species differ from Alpine varieties in its graceful shape and dark blue hues. This species is widely recognised for its medicinal properties, and it adds a distinctive bitter flavour to liqueurs.

Marsh Gladiolus
Gladiolus palustris
This is a very rare plant in Hungary, found individually in sandy flatlands. In Hungarian, it has attracted a variety of nick-names, such as "lad's flower", which attest to its aesthetic qualities.

Birdseye Primrose
Primula farinosa
There are over 500 varieties of primroses, most of which are yellow. This primrose is by contrast purple and one of the rarest in Hungary. Its Latin name derives from the flour like extract that can be made from its leaves. It is one of the most attractive rarities of the of the Káli basin.

Large Pink
Dianthus superbus

These basalt formations on St György's hill are among the most attractive geological phenomena in Hungary. The top of the hill is covered by a layer of hard basalt, almost 100 metres thick, which came to the surface a quarter of a million years ago. Erosion and other weather factors created these pillars, which resemble organ pipes. The summit of the hill offers a splendid view of the spectacular Tapolca basin.

The reeds of Little Balaton evokes the atmosphere of ancient swamps. This environment is a paradise of birds, and over two hundred and fifty different species have been observed.

Marsh Helleborine **Epipactus palustris**
Several new varieties and sub-varieties of helleborines have been described in Hungary in recent years, the most important of which being the bugaci variety. The marsh helleborine has a much longer history, and flourishes in hills, flatlands and on the edges of reeds. Pollination occurs through the agency of small airborne insects. Its flowers, when blown up by photography, evoke the contours of tropical orchids.

Balaton in the depths of winter: the sheets of ice on the water and the frozen forms on the shore epitomise the season.

The otter **Lutra Lutra**

The otter is found all over Eurasia, but its numbers are dwindling everywhere. It is rare in Hungary, mostly living at Balaton and South West Hungary. It is endangered by many factors since each otter inhabits a vast territory. It eats principally fish which it catches under the water. It is a skilful, almost artistic swimmer.

Mute Swan **Cygnus Olor**

These highly decorative and popular birds have begun arriving from the north in recent decades. Their numbers are on the increase, and they seem to flourish at Balaton. In winter, flocks of several hundred gather near the shore. In the breeding season, they form pairs and withdraw to their nesting sites.

St György Hill stands gleaming in the winter sunshine in the centre of the Tapolca basin, where many rare plants can be found.

***Bearded Tit* Panurus biaramicus**

The bearded tit is one of the jewels of the reeds. It gets its name from its colouring, which seems to bestow upon it a beard. It tends to rest on individual reeds, which bow down under its modest weight. Its makes its nests between the stumps, usually from dry reed leaves, which are also the colour of its tail.

Poplar trees along the shore of the Keszthely bay are one of the characteristic sights of the Balaton shore line.

THE DANUBE

Budapest with the Blue Danube in the foreground, the Buda Castle, part of the World Heritage, against the skyline, and on the left, the protected Gellért Hill.

Hungary's primary river. Its significance is shown by the fact that the whole country belongs to the catchment basin of the Danube, and the areas situated along the river have been, in the course of our history, the most fertile and most finely cultivated part of the country. The flood plains of the Danube and its tributaries are one of Hungary's greatest natural assets. There is an asset even under the riverbed – indeed, it is one of our greatest treasures: hidden beneath the pebbly bed is Europe's largest freshwater stock.

The Danube crosses the line of the Small Carpathians at Dévény. Leaving its precipitous upper sections, located in Germany and Austria, its gradient diminishes, with the river dividing itself into a thousand branches fanning out. Lying between the Moson Danube and the Old Danube is the Szigetköz. The Szigetköz is a unique portion of the Danube Valley – neither over it nor below it do we see a system of branches – formed on an alluvial cone – of this type.

The Szigetköz has produced an incredibly rich wildlife: it is home to more than 40 per cent of the entire Hungarian plant world, with a spectacularly high number of orchids, including twenty-four species. Eighty per cent of Hungary's dragon-fly and fish species, and nearly all the species of the amphibians are present. Because of their rarity, several hundred species of the representatives of the animal kingdom are included in the lists of the Red Books. The European beaver has once again established itself – spontaneously, probably from the Austrian stock. At the end of October, 1992, this rich wildlife was severely affected when Slovakia unilaterally diverted the waters of the Danube. It is the Fertő-Hanság National Park, in the Szigetköz Landscape Protection Area, that is responsible for the protection of the matchless assets of the Szigetköz.

It is at Esztergom that the Danube enters one of its most beautiful sections, the Danube bend, extending as far as Szentendre. This region owes its beauty to volcanic activity; the course of the Danube is intersected by the Börzsöny Mountains from the north and the Visegrád Mountains from the east – both of them andesite mountains. The river, forming terraces of gravel, gradually cut itself in among the mountains. Here, Nature has produced a most lavish collection of her gifts, in the form of surface formations and plant rarities. The wildlife of the Danube bend form a bridge between the Transdanubian and Northern Central Mountains, and between the submediterranean and continental boundaries.

Budapest, Hungary's capital city – of unique location and beauty – , is very rich in natural assets as well. The Castle Hill of Buda, which is a World Heritage site, the green belt of the city, Buda's thermal and karst springs and its medicinal waters, and the more than a hundred protected caves, are a unique natural asset. Gellért (St. Gerard) Hill and "Sas" (or "Eagle") Hill – also protected – are home to several rarities, including the yellow catchfly and the Pannonian lizard, which exclusively native to this area. It is the Duna-Ipoly National Park that is responsible for protecting the natural treasures of the Danube Bend and Buda Landscape Protection Area.

In the Danube Valley, Sárköz, lying below Paks, and the Mohács Island, lying below Baja, were once also a pristine acquatic world. This is the habitat of Hungary's strongest osprey and black stork population. Even today, the area is criss-crossed by channels. One of the outstanding assets of the Gemenc area is its red deer stock of excellent genetic quality and its wild boar population. Beavers, too, have been successfully reintroduced. On the gravel shelf of the Dráva river, the tern – very rare in Hungary – and the sandpiper have established themselves. Lake Riha is an important habitat of acquatic birds. The natural assets of this section of the rivers are overseen by the Danube-Dráva National Park.

Esztergom on the Danube Bend, which for more than two centuries, was the Royal Residence.

The twenty- to thirty-kilometre-wide flood-plain of the Danube cuts across Hungary as a green band visible from afar. As befits a great river, the trees in the flood-plains grow higher than elsewhere; and the vegetation of the flood-plains, too, are most luxuriant. The river and its tributaries, and the dead channels, are fringed by the foliage of the willows as a silver band, with groups of poplars on the banks and gallery forests of elms, ash-trees and oaks in the higher inundation areas. The flood-plains of the Danube and its tributaries are a paradise for migratory birds. At the time of the spring and autumn migrations, numerous flocks of whitethroats, chiffchaffs and blackbirds may be observed. On the dead channels, mortlakes and small lakes, we can admire the several-hundred-strong flocks of large egrettes, spoon-bills, common herons and black storks. In winter, tens of thousands of water birds can be sighted. For over a thousand years, the Danube Valley has been home to the Hungarian people. It provides rest and recreation for a growing number of people, offering unique experiences to fishing fans and the devotees of waters. To me, spring is the time when the flood-plains of the Danube are most beautiful: the alders, poplars, and willows open their red-white-green catkins; in the valley of the Danube, snow-white snowdrops, then sky-blue wild hyacinths, and later corydalises cover the forest floors. In the finest month, in May, we can walk in forests of lilies-of-the-valley. They remind one of the words of the director of nature films, István Homoki Nagy, who said: "Love the land where the lilies-of-the-valley open... The land where the dead foliage comes to new life, enveloping the banks of the big rivers in strident spring... These are most precious districts! ... for this is where we have the old Hungarian graves, now collapsed, and this is where the new Hungarian cradles are rocking..."

Dawn at Visegrad

At Szigetköz, the Danube has created a staggering natural phenomenon on gravel deposited over the centuries.

Great White Egret **Egretta alba**
The early Hungarians hunted the white egret for its feathers, which provided the plumage of princes and nobles. This egret is the true Snow White of the bird kingdom. It has been adopted as the symbol for Hungarian nature conservation. The strict laws governing its protection have been a success and the number of breeding pairs has increased each year. Today, there are several thousands of them.

At Szigetköz, artificial stone weirs in the flowing water guarantee the requisite water level for maintaining this microenvironment.

The Grey Heron

Ardea Cinerea

Youngsters waiting to be fed. Youngsters require a lot of food daily, usually fish. The grey heron is widespread throughout Eurasia, and in Hungary, tends to nest in high trees or reeds within the catchment areas of the Danube, Tisza and Dráva rivers. It is the most commonly observed species of heron.

Water Violet
Hottonia palustris
A meadow at Szigetköz. This is one of the most characteristic flowers in Hungary, found in clearings and marshlands. When the flowers all open together, it makes for a wonderful spectacle.

Lesser Butterfly Orchid **Platanthera bifolia**
This delicate, green and white flowered orchid is one of the more common to be found at Szigetköz

Common Twayblade **Listera ovata,**
with its characteristic form and green flowers

Among the more common flora on Szigetköz grow such rarities as the ***bee orchid*** **Ophyris apifera.** *Like other orchids, it does not flower every year, and in unfavourable years, remains under the ground. It only sprouts in rainy years. The shape of the flower is reminiscent of an insect in flight.*

The ***orange lily*** **Lilium bulbiferum** *is particularly striking to the eye and can be found at Szigetköz. It has been appropriated and cultivated by gardeners the world over.*

aThe beautiful ***Danube Carnation*** **Dianthus Collinus** *flourishes in the area of the Danube bend.*

One of Hungary's true natural treasures is the ***Freyer's Purple Emperor moth*** **Apatura metis** *which lives around the lower reaches of the Danube, and where the Dráva and Tisza meet. The females lay their eggs in the branches of willow trees, producing two generations per year, in June and August. It is a very rare moth and among the most beautiful.*

Linum dolomiticum

This plant was first discovered by the botanist Vince Borbás among the dolomite scree above the settlement of Pilisszentiván, and has been found nowhere else. This terrain hosts other rare flowers. The flower is very small indeed.

Ferula sadlerana

Another rarity among Hungarian flora can be found on one of the stone ledges of Gerecse. Its closest relatives can be found on the semi-desert steppelands of Asia. Its blooms can reach a height of more than a metre.

Visegrad is the jewel in the crown of the Danube bend. For several centuries, it was the capital of Hungary, and it enjoyed its zenith at the time of King Mátyás, who used it as a summer retreat. In 1483, a Papal delegation noted that "Visegrad is Heaven on Earth."

The Common Roller
Coracias garrulus
This species thrives in warm climates and is most common in Hungary around the Danube and Tisza rivers. The mating ritual of this species, with the male swooping down from on high at the female, which also demarcates his territory, leads to its English name, while its non-stop garrulous song leads to its Latin one. The pair declare their love publicly by sitting side by side, and bowing courteously to each other.

Bee eater

Merops apiaster

This bird most commonly nests in the Danube and Balaton regions, often in loess banks. The beauty of this bird has been much remarked upon through the centuries. "looking at its colour and appearance, it is as though it has not come from our climate, but from a climate far to the south, so beautiful and striking are its colours, and so unique its shape."

The untouched Gemenc area.

Gemenc is known the world over for its stunning scenery and the huge antlered deer. The superb wild meadows and pastures provide the nourishment for the growth of the Gemenc deers' vast, dark coloured antlers.

The finest stock of fallow deer in the world has made the Gyulaj forest famous.

***The Osprey* Haliaeetus ablicilla**
One of the great success stories of Hungarian conservation has been the Osprey protection program, launched in 1986. It has succeeded in raising the number of nesting couples to over a hundred. They nest in the uninhabited forests of South West Hungary and Somogy county, as well as the Danube and Dráva catchment area. In recent years, nesting pairs have been observed in Bakony and Hortobágy in East Hungary.

The Black Stork **Ciconia nigra**

Unlike the white stork, this bird is a timid, cautious bird, which makes its nest far from human habitats. In Hungary, they can be found hidden away in the South, in the Danube's catchment area and alongside the larger tributaries. They nest in old oaks and grey poplar trees.

The section of the Danube bend alongside Visegrád and Nagymaros is one of the most beautiful areas of countryside in the world.

Duna at Moson in winter

THE TISZA

The Szabolcs mound on the Tisza shore, built when the Hungarians first invaded this area.

I am partial to the Tisza, since I grew up on the bank of its largest tributary, the Bodrog. The river Tisza is Hungary's second largest river, and the tenth largest river in Europe. In world terms, however, it is really a small river. Still, to us, the Tisza means more than mere figures; it is a genuine Hungarian river, originating and flowing into the Danube in the territory of historical Hungary. The Tisza and its tributaries are, throughout, accompanied by the anxious love of Hungarians. From its river-head, it brings the message of the Carpathians; everywhere, its waves are churned up by the wishes of Hungarians. Nearly half of Hungary's population lives within the orbit of the Tisza, with the other half having some sort of connection with the river. When we see its dear banks, overgrown with willows, or maybe just hear about the "fair" Tisza, our Hungarian hearts beat faster – we tend to think of it the way a parent thinks of his fondest child.

To understand the more recent problems relating to the Tisza, we have to acquaint ourselves with what happened in the past. The ancient flood-plains of the Tisza and its tributaries used to measure exactly two million hectares, amounting to a quarter of Hungary's total land area. In Roman times, the valley of the Tisza was still described as "a region full of marshes". The Hungarian tribes who came here during Árpád's conquest of our homeland were attracted by the rich pastures of the Tisza, irrigated by floods and made fertile by the silt of the rivers, and by the fabulous possibilities for hunting and fishing. But, despite all its riches, the Tisza became a hindrance to the economic development of the region, as the unregulated river used an enormous flood-plain which would have been suitable for agricultural production as well. Slowly, the idea matured of regulating the waters of the Tisza. Count István Széchenyi was the intellectual author of the project, with Pál Vásárhelyi put in charge of drawing up the plans. From 1846 to 1872, from Tiszaújlak to Titel, running at a 138-kilometre-long section, 107 through-cuts were made on the Tisza, shortening the river by 510 kilometres.

To the Hungarian people, the water regulation project amounted to something of a second Conquest in terms of the dividends it paid, since an area of a million hectares were secured against the floods, making them available for farming. Even at that early stage, the Dutch hydraulic engineer Overmars drew attention to the need to afforest the slopes of the Carpathians and to plant them with grass, and to construct water reservoirs on the upper section of the Tisza and its tributaries; his advice is still correct and would be worth taking even today. The highest water levels measured before the regulation of the river were around 600 cm. After the river regulation, the level gradually rose, so that, by the end of the millennium, the

Tisza was already nearing the 1100 cm mark. It seems we have taken away too much area from the Tisza, so the river is now reclaiming its due ever more spectacularly. In January, 2000, the Tisza was hit by a cyanide spill of disastrous proportions; and, not much later, it also became polluted with heavy metal silt. Everybody hurried to save the river, but still, it was the Tisza itself that did the most to help itself. In April, the Tisza reached an unprecedentedly high water level, causing it to "shake hands" with the Bodrog at Zalkod. The two rivers combined with a huge volume of water and an enormous quantity of silt, has washed away the pollution, replacing the unparalleled wildlife from the water of the dead channels, the mortlakes, the Tisza lake and the tributaries.

The Tákos church, with its handcarved wooden interior

This wildlife is invaluable, since the Tisza and the floodplain connected with it, along with the dead channels, are one of the most important natural assets not only of Hungary, but of Europe as a whole, too. The natural beauties of the river begin right after it enters Hungary. The present-day picture of this area is similar to what it was in the old days, with willow shrubbery fringing the living bed, gallery forests of willows and poplars of exquisite beauty, and woods of ash-trees, elms, English oaks and grey poplars and patches of hornbeams in the higher floodplains. In the central Tisza region, the river has many sharp twists and turns, its banks are fringed by beautiful willows and white and black poplars. This is where the bird reserve of Pély is situated, with the protected areas of Óballa and Vezseny, and the sand martin colony of Tiszakécske. Of the dead channels, the most beautiful ones are the Göbe, the Csatló, and the Cserőköz dead channel. The construction of the hydroelectric power plant at Kisköre produced the Tisza lake, which, with its rich wildlife, has become a very important area. In the Lower Tisza District, the principal assets were placed under the Mártély and Pusztaszer Landscape Protection Areas. The area owes its richness to the fact that this is the meeting-point of the wildlife of the "Duna-Tisza köz" – the central region lying between the Danube and the Tisza – and the "Tiszántúl" – i.e. Transdanubia. Embedded in the Landscape protection Area is the Ópusztaszer National Memorial Park, where the exhibitions of the Church of Forests showcase Hungary's natural endowments.

The marvellous wildlife of the Tisza belong to the Hortobágy, the Kiskunság, and the Körös-Maros National Parks; but the living Tisza also needs our own protective vigilance and stewardship. We share the responsibility for the Tisza with the neighbouring countries, as its catchment area is shared by five countries, with nearly half of its area located in Romania.

In conversation then I asked my kin:
"Why is the Tisza blamed, what is her sin?
She is accused of every wrong and dearth –
Yes she's the tames river on the earth."

A few days later as I slept carefree,
The tolling bells' alarm awakened me:
'The water comes! The flood! To higher ground!"
I saw an ocean when I looked around.

And like a madman tearing off his chain,
The Tisza galloped hard across the plain:
Screaming and roaring she broke her dams
and whirled –
She was intent to swallow all the world.

PETŐFI – THE TISZA

The upper reaches of the Tisza are characterised by flat, narrow and sometimes stony channels, and many deposits. Ferenc Kölcsey, who wrote the poem that is now the text of the Hungarian national anthem, grew up in this area at the turn of the 19th century at Szatmárcseke, and wrote that this area is "hidden away. It is beautiful but wild and extremely lonely. The Tisza flows from one direction, the Túr from the other … and leaves us to live in the delta."

Spring Snowflake
Leucojum vernum
This plant occurs frequently in the upper reaches of the Tisza and in Western Hungary. It flowers in early spring, favouring wet ground in woods of hornbeam, oak, as well as marshland. It blossoms at the start of March, and its bending, white flowers with green spots are truly the harbinger of spring.

The Carpathian Saffron

Crocus heuffelianus

Saffrons are principally a Mediterranean species. They are mentioned in the Bible and on Egyptian papyruses. The Carpathian saffron is found in the Carpathian mountains and those in the Balkans. They seem to have arrived in Hungary following the paths of mountain waters and can now be found in the hornbeam and oak woods in Szatmár-Bereg, East Hungary.

Fritillary

Fritillaria meleagris

This rarity grows in marshlands and wet woodland. It usually flowers before Easter and people used to pick these bell shaped, gracefully bent, chequered flowers and weave them into bunches. The fritillary is known by many different names in Hungarian, including "chess board lily".

The Tisza at Olcsvaapáti

The ***May Fly*** **Palingenia longicauda,** *is one of the hallmarks of the river Tisza. It is one of the largest and most attractive of the European ephemoptera species. At around six in the evening, they magically surface as nymphs, and after a quick shedding, fly to the shore, where they shed once again, attaching themselves to a variety of objects. They then fly over the water. The numerous long tailed males pursue the relatively few females, and great clusters form. Mating occurs amid a characteristic dance. When it gets dark, the females fly in swarms of tens of thousands at tree level, in the opposite direction of the river's flow, and scatter their eggs. After mating, the exhausted males rapidly die, and soon, the river is covered with their bodies. The next day, it is only the shed skins, still clinging to the vegetation on the shore, that remind us of this spectacular event.*

Washland willows in spring

The lesser Túr flows peacefully into the river Tisza

King Fisher

Alcedo atthis

This most loved of birds can be found in Hungary too. In flight, it creates the impression of being a blue jewel. Its underbelly resembles the colour of a dried leaf, which perhaps makes it easier to take the fish that it eats by surprise. From above, it blends in with the flowing stream, thus protecting it from hawks.

Fishermen rarely come home empty handed after a day by the Tisza. Traditional Tisza fishermen bring only a net, which they fix to freshly cut branches, and then cast it deep into the water, using an action inherited from their ancestors.

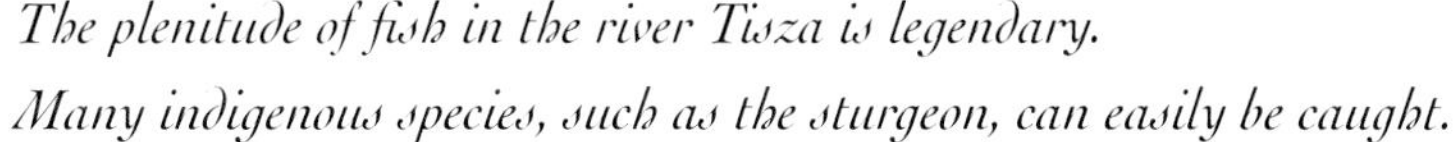

The plenitude of fish in the river Tisza is legendary.
Many indigenous species, such as the sturgeon, can easily be caught.

The Tisza ferries are indispensable for those who fish on the river.

Fringed Water Lily
Nymphoides peltata

There are breathtakingly beautiful colonies of this plant on the Tisza lake. Between the emerald green, circular, reflective leaves, the gossamer golden yellow flower open. This water lily can be found in dead channels along the Danube and Drava rivers as well.

The White Water Lily
Nymphaea alba

This well known attractive plant thrives in a scattering of places in Hungary. It flourishes best in relatively shallow, slow moving river, and the best examples can be found in the dead channels of the river Tisza. The flowers shut at night, and open their porcelain white petals in the morning sunshine.

The ***whiskered tern.*** **Chlidonas hybrida**
This bird nests in the river flats, lagoons and flat land lakes. Terns keep an almost permanent aerial watch over the water, swooping down occasionally to catch the insects they feed on. Mating only begins once the warm weather has arrived in June. They line their nest with weeds. They tend to nest in colonies, sometimes with grebes.

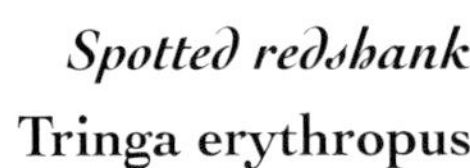

Spotted redshank
Tringa erythropus
The redshank does not nest in Hungary, but can be seen during its spring and autumn migrations in the vicinity of the river Tisza. The spotted redshank can sometimes be observed in flocks and even in pairs.

***Avocet* Recurvirostra avosetta**

This species nests in countless places along the European coast and only rarely inland. However, an exception is Hungary where they always nest principally alongside saline lakes. They make for a spectacular sight in early spring, as they search for food with scything movements of their heads. However, their mating dance is even more fascinating, and after mating, they embrace each other, and entwine their necks, and race forwards in this position for many metres.

The ***black legged stilt*** **Himantopus Himantopus**

This bird requires a warm climate and only arrive in Hungary at the end of April. Once they have settled, they quickly set about starting families, after performing a spectacular mating ritual. The hen, producing a very attractive song, keeps its neck above the water, and in this position invites her partner. The male always approaches her from the side, splashes her with water, and strokes her back with his neck. After mating, they entwine their necks, and with a graceful motion, confirm that they are now a pair.

Little Egret **Egretta garzetta**
It Hungary, it lives primarily alongside the Tisza. It makes its nest in flood plains and forests. It frequently changes its nesting places, and often settles in nesting colonies along with herons. It has been described as the ballerina of the bird kingdom, thanks to its graceful movements. Its two decorative feathers on its head, and others on its back and rear, make it particularly beautiful.

Squacco heron **Ardeola ralloides**
This is a relatively small heron. When it is disturbed, it stands up stiffly and thrusts its head above the greenery to see what is going on. Its white neck makes a stark contrast with the surrounding greenery. It often nests along with larger herons.

Red-Footed Falcon **Falco vespertinus**

The male is pale grey, with lively chestnut red thighs and tail base, while around its eyes and feet, it is red. The male eats only insects and beetles.

In April 2000, the Tisza and Bodrog rivers were at their highest levels for over a century, and there was immense flooding. Whole areas of East Hungary resembled a sea, and from this picture, we can only guess where the Bodrog river bed actually is.

The Bodrog before it joins the Tisza at Tokaj. At Szegi, it snakes around the hills. The water level is usually low and this photo presents an idyllic image of the river.

The meeting of the Tisza and Bodrog rivers at Tokaj

A carpet of ***Water Chestnuts*** **Trapa natans,** *in a Tisza dead channel at Mártély. This plant is a member of the family of weeds that flourish in standing waters, and occurs most frequently along the Tisza. It is an indicator of biological cleanness, and does not occur at all to the west. In the Middle Ages, during times of famine, people would dry and grind it as a substitute for flour.*

Chrysanthemum serotinum
It blossoms at the end of summer, and its white petals make it stand out from among the other plants and flowers. It can only be found in isolated examples, and never grows together.

The river Tisza and its shore, illuminated by the autumn sun. The dawn frosts have already taken a toll on the poplar trees' leaves, but before winter finally sets in, yellow ivy leaves, climbing up trees and bushes, shine in their full effulgent beauty.

The shoreline woods and willows produce a picturesque winter scene.

The splendour of the Tisza in spring, summer and autumn is replaced with splendour of a different kind.

THE MOUNTAINS

Hollókő

Although the highest mountains of Hungary do not reach the majesty of the Himalayas or the breathtaking beauty of the Alps, the territory of historical Hungary, wreathed with the Carpathian Mountains, must have been one of the most scenic landscapes in the globe. The poet Sándor Petőfi had just reason to say: "...if this earth is God's hat, our country is the bouquet on it!" Of this princely gift, we have been left with the centre or the heart of the Carpathian Basin and the Northern Central Mountains, the southern rim portion of the Carpathians. Another legacy we have received, in the Carpathian Basin, is that – thanks to our geographical situation – we see a great variety of plant and animal species – we have great "biodiversity", to use a fashionable word -, with a cooccurrence of species of different origin and many aboriginal or autochthonal species. That is the treasure representing our real wealth. Let's set out from the east and review our treasures. Rising in the eastern corner of the country are the Zemplén Mountains, which are one of Hungary's most scenic and richest regions – richest, that is, in terms of its natural assets, a region still intact. Plant rarities include the mountain anemone; while, looking at the bird population, almost all the owl species hatching in Hungary have nested in this area.

In the Aggtelek karst region, nearly all the forms of karst phenomena can be observed; the karst plateaus segmented by dolinas, the rows of sink-holes, the several-kilometre-long limestone canyons are among the most beautiful karst phenomena in the world. The variety and unspoilt character of the cave world of the Aggtelek and the Slovak karst are unique in Europe, with an unparalleled wealth of forms shaping the stalactites and stalagmites; 20 of the 27 dripstone forms described until now are evident here. The cave system is home to over five hundred animal species, including some that are unique to this site, such as the Hungarian blind carabus or the Aggtelek blind crab. Living on the surface there are some plant rarities. Based on all these, the cave world of the Aggtelek and the Slovak karst were declared a World heritage site in 1995, what's more, in the "rare natural" category. The Bükk is the most picturesque portion of the Northern Central Mountains, one of the highest karstic plateaus of Hungary. Its surface is segmented by dolinas, swallowholes, ravines, and rocks of the most diverse forms. No less varied than the surface configurations is the vegetation cover of the Bükk. Those rare plants are the most precious which have survived in the frost-pocket dolinas or cool valleys, such as the yellow violet and the meadow sword-grass. As regards its fauna, the yellow-and-black-spotted land-salamander, the alpine newt and the Hungarian barbel are some of the most noteworthy species.

Hollókő is a real jewel, situated in the depths of the Cserhát Mountains. In 1989, UNESCO –

because of the exemplary preservation of the "Ófalu" (Old Village), the traditional farming methods, the still vibrant cultural traditions and folk costumes of the village – included Hollókő in the World Heritage list. The natural plant cover of the Mátra is formed by oak- and beech-woods. Geo-botanically, it is regarded as a special region – "Mátra flora district"; it provides a habitat for some rare alpine plants native to the Carpathians. The Börzsöny, nestling in the arc of the Ipoly, is one of Hungary's most scenic districts. It is a mountain range with a centrifugal network of valleys, with three hundred and fifty springs rising in its area.

Crossing the line of the Danube, we come to the districts of the Dunántúl (Transdanubian) Central Mountains. The Gerecse and the Vértes mainly consist of dolomite; the erosion of the surface has produced sheer rocky walls and ravines. The mountains are covered by oak-woods – naturally hungry for lime – and, in the south-eastern parts, by karstic scrub forests of Hungarian fustic, which turn red in autumn. Their plant rarity is the submediterranean eastern hornbeam. The imperial eagle and the lanner constantly nest here. The greater part of the Bakony – and, more particularly, of the "Öreg" (Old) Bakony – is covered with original hornbeam- and beech-woods, with many brook valleys in their depths: the valleys of the Gerence and the Cuha streams are the finest. Alongside its plant rarities, we also find here some rare animals, including the whiskered bat and the water bat; while the white-backed wood-pecker is native to this area only.

The Abbey of Pannonhalma is perched atop a triple hill of exquisite beauty, in the northern part of the Bakony. It was in 996 that Prince Géza, father to St. Stephen settled the Benedictine monks here. To all our delight, the Abbey of Pannonhalma was adopted, in 1996, as a World Heritage site.

Pannonhalma

The Mecsek combines all of Hungary's bio-geographical attributes; at the same time, it is home to some extremely rare plant and animal species. Sársomlyó – covered with multiple layers of limestone – rises almost as an island from the adjacent hilly district. Thanks to its submediterranean climate, it has a uniquely rich flora; in Hungary, it is the only habitat of the Hungarian wild saffron and numerous other rarities.

The Kőszeg Mountains, segmented by the Sopron valley and some deep valleys, is located in one of Hungary's westernmost sectors; and, in terms of its wildlife, it already belongs to the foot of the Alps.

Virtually all of Hungary's national parks – including the Bükk, the Aggtelek, the Danube-Ipoly, the Balaton Uplands, the Danube-Dráva, and the Fertő-Hanság National Parks – involve themselves in the preservation of the natural treasures of our mountains.

The area of Zemplén, with its meadow flowers in May, its emerald green woods and castle remains from the Árpád era at Füzér make it one of the most enchanting areas of countryside in Hungary.

The Cuba stream, one of many that flow through the deep valley of the Bakony's untouched beech wood forests.

***Auricula* Primula auricula subsp. hungarica**

This has one of the most striking colours – golden yellow -of all the primroses that grow in the wild. It can be found in north facing crevices that virtually never see the light of day. Its leaves resemble a bear's ear, which is how it is known in folk culture. It is one of the remaining plants that flourished here at the time of the ice-age.

Lanner **Falco cherrug**
This bird is often associated with the turul bird which features prominently in Hungarian mythology. It is also one of the success stories of Hungarian nature conservation. According to the writer Anonymous, the mother of one of the original Hungarian tribe leaders, Álmos, was made pregnant by a lanner, and from her sprang a noble line of kings. Hungarian legend says it was a turul bird that guided the migrating Hungarians to the Carpathian basin where they settled. Lanners nest all the way from China to the Carpathian basin. They are declining in number everywhere except in Hungary, where in recent years, their number have grown four fold. The Hungarian Ornithological Association symbolically celebrated the year 2000 by naming it the year of the lanner.

At Aggtelek, on the side of Tóhegy, can be found one of Hungary's landscape treasures – the karren-feld, which is known in folk culture as "the devil's tilled field." In the place of the roots of felled trees the rock bed was revealed, and thus the porous, grooved karren-feld was formed.

Dripstones in the Baradla cave.

The action of rain water sinking into the ground eroded the underlying rock, making cavities and sometimes, immense caves, together with an array of dripstones. The beauty of these stones has been increased by coloured materials that were dissolved in the water.

The Red lake with the Bear Cliffs.

***Tornaian Golden Drap* Onosma tornense**

One of the great figures of Hungarian botany, Sándor Jávorka, discovered this plant in 1906. It is one of the rarest plants in the whole of Europe. It can only be found among the Torna kaste stone, both in Hungary and over the border in Slovakia.

***Teleki flower* Telekia speciosa**

The distinguished researcher into the flora of Transylvania, J. Ch. Baumgarten, was the first to note this large, exceptionally beautiful plant, and he named it after Count Teleki, the chancellor of Transylvania. It is known in not just Hungary, but in the Alps, Carpathians, Transylvania and Caucasus. In the picture, a red admiral butterfly is paying a visit.

Lady's Slipper Orchid
Cypripedium calcedus
This orchid occurs across a wide area of Northern Eurasia. It lives among the kaste oak forests. It is one of the most attractive orchids to be found in Hungary. Its slipper shaped flowers entice insects which inadvertently pollinate it. The World Wildlife Fund has declared this orchid to be one of the most endangered species in the world.

Kopasz hill, near Tokaj, bears grapes that make the famous wine, and this hill is even mentioned in the Hungarian national anthem. This volcanic formation is the tallest of its kind in Hungary and hosts many rare plants and animals on its slopes.

Rock Thrush **Monticola saxatilis**
The size of a thrush, but slightly shorter, its head, neck and chest down to the breast are ash blue, while its belly is a rust colour. It jumps well and feeds on spiders, flies and beetles. Its song is variable, as with all thrushes, and seems almost flute like.

Astragalus dasyanthus

The majority of these plants occur in Hungary, with a scattering in neighbouring countries. It flourishes best near Danube and Tisza. It is nonetheless a rarity in Tokaj.

Globeflower **Trollius europaeus**

The yellow sea of globeflowers on the scree slopes of the still snow-capped Carpathians, Alps and Dolomites is one of the most splendid sights of early spring. Its presence in Western Hungary and the Nyírség region in the east is a harbinger of the impending mountains. These flowers are particularly striking in the Bakony mountains.

Peony Paeonia banatica

Peony, the name given to this family of plants, is named after the Greek Goddess of healing. Its curative properties are far exceeded by its external appearance: it is one of the most striking sights in May in the Mecsek mountains. Efforts of conservationists have concentrated on this plant. It has been present in this area since before the last ice-age. It can be found in Mecsek, Serbia and Slovenia.

***Sowbread* Cyclamen purpurascens**

"The most beautiful jewel of the Sopron woods in the cyclamen. When its five part corona light up the forest in August, it marks the high point of the seasons' circular progress."

REZSŐ BECHT: SOPRONI SEASONS

***Great Meadow Rue* Thalictrum aquilegiifolium**

This plant is prominent in May in Mecsek. Its unmistakable, large flowers are like fireworks exploding in the sky, and open one after the other. They live in the kaste forests.

Monkey Orchid
Orchis simia
This variety of orchid is very rare, occuring only in Mecsek and the Villányi hills. The plant obtains its name from the shape of its flowers. It seems to have arrived in Hungary before the last ice-age.

Austrian Golden Drap
Dracocephalum austriacum
This plant grows from the Pirenese to the Causasian mountains, and can be found in Austria, Slovakia and around Torda. In Hungary, it has only been observed in the Torda carst.

Colchicum hungaricum

This is one of the rarest plants in Hungary. In mild winters, it can even flower in January. Its petals are white or a faint amethyst-violet. Its only grows at Szársomlyó in Hungary. It was discovered by the botanist Viktor Janka in 1867, and was declared a protected species in 1944, making it one of the first subjects of Hungarian conservationism.

Digitalis ferruginea

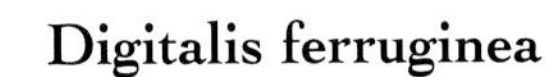

Its relative, foxglove, has been used for centuries for combating heart problems and for curing animals. The leaves of digitalis ferruginea also contain the necessary chemical but its rarity prevents its exploitation. It is very endangered because of the coal mining at Szársomlyó.

Coal mining has gouged deep wounds into the eastern and western sides of Szársomlyó, which is covered with multiple layers of limestone. Here we can see the grapes which go to produce the famous Villány wines, as well as new settlements

Dipper **Cinclus Cinclus**

This bird hunts in the most unusual fashion – it perches on a stone or other solid object in a fast flowing stream, and then dives in, and manages to "fly" upstream, in its hunt for underwater creatures. It is noted for its persistence.

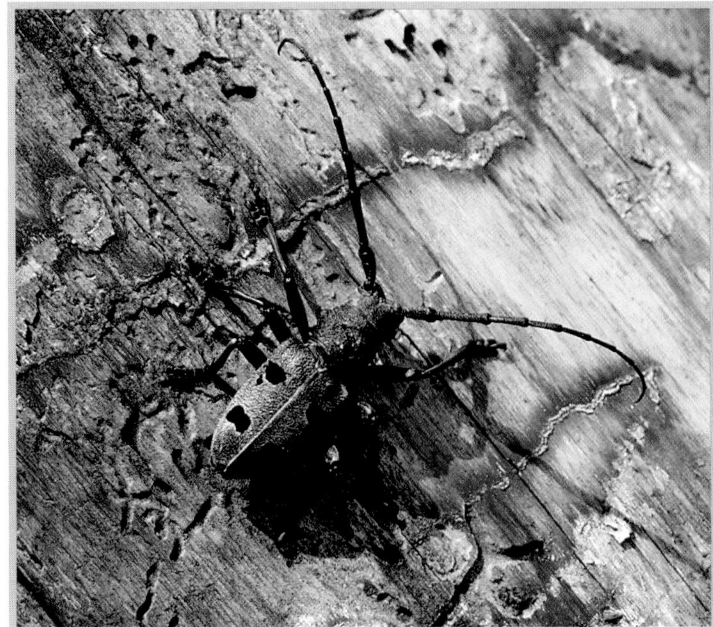

Morimus funereus

This beetle is wide spread, from Spain to the Balkans. In Hungary, it lives in beech groves, its larvae grow in old trees and logs. The species is currently endangered.

The ancient splendour of the Mátra mountains surrounded by the houses of Parádsasvár.

The first snowfall in the Bükk mountains

Morning autumn mists on the Medves plain

The linden walk at Nagycenk.

The grandfather of Count István Széchenyi planted 645 linden trees along a two and a half kilometre stretch between his mansion at Nagycenk and the shore at Fertőd. The trees made a road that was 20 metres apart, suitable for driving, riding and even sledge rides. Over the years, most of the original trees have been replaced with large leaved lindens. In June, the odour of the blossom enchants visitors, but winter snowfalls can leave a similar impression. Hungary hopes that this linden walk will soon become part of the World Heritage.

THE PUSZTA

The Fás puszta near Bélmegyer evokes steppe woodlands

One of Hungary's most characteristic regions is the puszta (the Hungarian "steppe"), which, to those arriving from other countries, can provide – after the cultured regions variegated with woods and fields – a completely different world. The aspect of the puszta changes from season to season, but it is in winter that its real face becomes visible. The landscape becomes almost arctic. The poet Sándor Petőfi was right when he said, "Oh but the waste has been laid waste with a vengeance!" At such times, the cold breaths of the scenic puszta cut to the bone; you get frequent hard frosts with hoar-frost. Chilly winds and blizzards reign supreme in the puszta, with ribs of snow and ice ploughing the landscape in their wake. Both man and beast seek shelter.

The February sunshine soon breaks the strength of winter; the ice starts to melt, and wild waters flood the earth in ever larger areas. The sunshine soon revitalises the puszta, the grass starts growing, and the more restless among the grey cattle and sheep now crave the pastures. The flocks of wild geese and wild ducks appear, with the first groups of lapwings. In March flowers start to emerge in a still colourless puszta. Numerous groups of redshanks, with their jingling voices, godwits ruffs arrive at the soggy meadows. The Lenten winds bring, in good order, the storks and the flocks of spoon-bills to the reeds. In the middle of April, the bustard cocks rutting in the puszta appear, their feather roses visible from a long distance. April and May are months of rich pastures. The buttercups and irises open their petals; everywhere birds performing their mating dances are to be seen. Everywhere, the bird hotels of the puszta fill with migrants and non-migrants alike. After St. George's day, the bluebell already heralds the coming of Easter. Early in May, we can admire flowery meadows of Transylvanian plantain and camomile. In spring, the puszta receives its beauty from the picturesque meadow foxtail. In the Kiskunság district, thousands of acacias blossom, and the wind of the puszta flutters needlegrass in the sandy meadows. In summer, it is the big storms that bring some refreshment into the sweltering heat. At the end of August, the storks already gather together, preparing for the big journey. Autumn finds only yellow fields after the abundance of spring and summer. Soon the landscape assumes an even homelier, pale-brown garb, tufts of gossamer fly and then settle in all parts of the puszta. Mysterious autumn fogs descend onto the landscape, with the hoarfrost an ever more frequent visitor at dawn. In October, small flocks of dotterels arrive from the northern tundras, and the migration of the cranes – one of the greatest spectacles the puszta has to offer – begins. The frosts of November sweep away even the last representatives of the cranes; the snow-buntings arrive, and the eryngos are now the only thing that the cold northern winds chase.

The golden era of Hungary's pusztas began in the 1700s, when Debrecen owned the Hortobágy, and Kecskemét was master of the puszta plains of the Kiskunság district, both cities developing a model farming economy of detached farmsteads and a pasturage-based livestock-breeding sector. In those times, Hungary was the top country in the world in terms of the number of livestock per capita. Everywhere, there were flocks of sheep – their sheep-bells ringing – and horse herds grazing in the fields. At that time, thousands of the world-famous Hungarian grey cattle would still be driven to Western European slaughterhouses. Everywhere in the puszta, you would see whitewashed farmsteads and herdsman's huts, with the sounds of happy music heard from inside the ("csárda") country taverns. It was this fairy-tale world that the poet Sándor Petőfi was still witness to, allowing him to capture it in his poems. No less rich, in those days, were the wildlife and the natural wealth of the puszta. After many trials and tribulations, the wildlife has, at last, found protection in the areas of the national parks. The population of rare birds – including aquatic warblers and lanners – has multiplied; while the stock of spoonbills and herons nesting among the reeds is now almost what it was in those early days; and the white-winged terns are seen nesting in the watery areas by the thousand – an unprecedented figure for this species. Of the Transylvanian plantain and the meadow aster, only a couple of stems were to be found in the puszta two decades ago; now you get hundreds of thousands of these plants. And the number of cranes – which migrate in autumn and stay here for weeks – is now nearing the one hundred thousand mark.

Ópusztaszer plays a central role in early Hungarian history

But what is the peculiar value of the puszta rooted in? The unbroken horizon, the boundlessness of the puszta evoke a sense of human freedom – a freedom without bounds, almost an emblem of the untrammelled soaring of human thoughts. This is where the sunrises and the sunsets are the most beautiful; the mirage (or Fata Morgana) brings to the residents of these parts their wishes, too, in the shape of green gardens, farmsteads and wells. The brilliance of the starry sky is there to enjoy almost in its entirety, with neither tall buildings nor mountains to intercept the view of the spectacle. On cloudless nights, the Milky Way shines in its full beauty. The puszta offers a home to its plants so they can unfold their flowery meadows, providing its birds with paradisic abundance with a constantly well-laid table, and ensuring a livelihood for the people of the puszta – representing a real asset for Hungary. As of 1999, the Hortobágy has been a World Heritage site as well. In the Hortobágy, Kiskunság, and the Körös-Maros National Parks, our rare treasures are jealously guarded.

The Hungarian Puszta, or Great Plain, has inspired great works of Hungarian literature and art.

Colonies of scented mayweed are one of the defining spectacles of the Puszta. This plant will not grow in the lower wetlands, nor the higher plateaus. However, when the altitude is right it grows in abundance, and seems like a river snaking across the land. Besides its aesthetic aspects, is a very much used medicinal herb.

When it is in flower, the ***Stone Curlew*** **Burhinus oedicnemus** *is sitting in its nest. During the day, it is almost immobile among the greenery, but at night it is active, searching for food and frequently letting out a distinctive call. It is a rare nesting bird in Hungary, preferring true bare sub-desert and sandy desert environments. It flourishes in the Sahara. In Hungary it can be found in the sandy land of Kiskunság, in Maros-Körös and on the Hortobágy Puszta.*

The ***Great Bustard*** **Otis tarda,** *was chosen as the symbol for the Hungarian Ornithological and Nature Conservation Association. The largest population in Europe is to be found in Hungary, which is a tribute to the work of conservationists. There is a special bustard unit functioning at Dévaványy, where rescued eggs are hatched and stray chics reared. The mating dance in April is a sight worth seeing. The cocks fly at dawn to their favoured places, and then fan out their entire plumage. They blow up their immense necks and bend them backwards in an arc, to show their feathers to the best advantage. The high point of the ritual comes when the hen approaches.*

Aquatic Warbler **Acrocephalus paludicola**
Hungary is one of the few countries in Europe where this bird nests. Its territory extends around Hortobágy. It favours wet territory with fresh, marsh grasses. Special drainage schemes have resulted in the Aquatic Warbler's territory being dramatically expanded over recent years.

Adonis transsylvanicus
This is one of the rarest flowers in Hungary, and every centimetre where it grows deserves our protection. It occurs in just two areas of meadow and outside Hungary, it only grows in Northern Romania, but even then, in small numbers.

Sand Iris
Iris humilis
Arenaria
This rare iris grows in sandy plains.

The Puszta offers an infinite variety of colours and patterns of blossoming flowers.

The Kun mounds are one of the unique treasures of the Carpathian Basin. There are almost forty thousand on the Puszta. These mounds were created by peoples living in the area before the Hungarians arrived, and were used as look out mounds or for burials. Later, they marked territorial borders. They are now most important for scenic, archaeological and biological reasons. Each one has a name and people living here use them for navigational purposes. Several rare plants grow on them. In the picture, we see the Csipő mound.

Bulbocodium vernum

Along with the spotted saffron, this is the earliest flowering plant in Hungary. In the Carpathian basin, it occupies the sandy plains of the Nyírség region and the those of Duna Tisza region. It also occurs in Transsylvania in Romania.

***Ophrys scolopax* subspecies cornuta**

The orchids of the Western Mediterranean are a rarity in the Danube Tisza region. Conservationists have preserved a population of several thousand. The flowers of this species produce a sex pheromone, which along with the shape of the flower, persuades insects to mate with it. In this way, it achieves its real aim of exchanging pollen with other members of its own species.

Pulsatilla patens

This is another early flowerer. It is found in sandy meadows and grassy steppelands, particularly in Poland and Russia. In Hungary, it only occurs in the Nyírség region in East Hungary.

Hungarian Iris
Iris aphylla subsp. hungarica
This iris was discovered at Hegyalja by the distinguished polymath, Pál Kitaibel, who described it in his book Descriptiones et icones plantarum rariorum Hungariae. It can also be found in a few areas of North East Hungary, in rocky and sandy terrains. This plant only occurs in the Carpathian Basin.

Zephyr Blue **Plebejides pyalon**
This rare butterfly can be found in the Kiskunság Plane and the sandy meadows of Somlyó. Its caterpillars feed on plants that are also a protected species. The grubs feed on the leaves and flowers, and secretes a sweet substance, much appreciated by ants, who in turn then leave it alone.

The Sand Hillocks at Fülöpháza

These sand mounds, that can be found in the Danube Tisza region, are blown and rearranged by the wind. These sand hillocks are surrounded by interesting grasses.

***Snounted Grasshopper* Acrida hungarica**
This is technically a locust and is the only such species to live in Hungary. The snouted grasshopper requires a high temperature and earth warmed through by the sun. As a result, it only develops at the end of summer. It can be found in the sandy planes of the Kiskun and Nyírség areas.

Meadow Viper
Vipera ursinii
This poisonous snake is one of the rarest and most endangered snakes in Europe. It was first described by Lajos Méhely in 1893. It can be found in damp meadows but prefers higher land. The fate of this animal depends very much on that of the Hungarian colony. It is known to exist only in the Hanság and Kiskunság areas.

Storm on the Puszta

***White-winged Black Tern* Chlidonias leucopterus**
This tern is established only in the very East of the country. It has only passed the Western bank of the Tisza in recent years. It is a bird particularly pleasing to the eye. It returns to its territory in early May, when the mating season begins. One of the actions of the mating dance is the male offering his would be bride food.

***Eared Grebe* Podiceps nigricollis**
This grebe enjoys warm climates and only occurs in South Hungary. It makes its nest in its territory, which it continually changes. It seems happiest nesting along with other terns. It even constructs nests that float on the water, from weeds and other plant material.

Red-breasted grebe **Podiceps griseigena**
This is the rarest of the grebes that breed in Hungary. Its mating dance is particularly spectacular, and the pairs will swim together side by side, and then after gathering nesting material onto the necks, touch each other's backs, and both rise from the water and run on its surface, in a manner reminiscent of penguins.

Glossy Ibis **Plegadis falcinellus**
In Europe, this bird nests always in the vicinity of water. It was wide spread in Hungary, until various drainage schemes begun last century, drastically reduced its habitat. Between 1953 and 1984, it was not observed in Hungary, until one was seen at Hortobágy. Since then, the number of breeding pairs has increased, and its nesting sights are very strictly protected and left alone.

Saline plain at Hortobágy. Salt and soda have come to the surface, whitening the soil. Only very specialised plants and animals can live in this terrain.

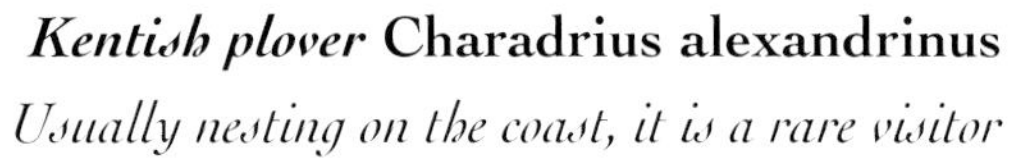

Kentish plover **Charadrius alexandrinus**
Usually nesting on the coast, it is a rare visitor to inland Europe. It enjoys bare, forbidding environments. Its shape and colour enables it to blend in most convincingly. The decline in such environments has led to a steady decline in its numbers.

Short-toed lark **Calandrella brachydactyla**
This bird only nests in Hungary and for this reason, attracts ornithologists from all over the world. It has a variety of behaviours that make the effort of tracking it down worth while, for example, its habit of swooping down from on high while singing its characteristic song. It is very strictly protected.

Collared pratincole **Glareola pratincola**
We see a chick looking desperately for its parents. This bird is also steadily declining in numbers. Formerly, there were substantial colonies on the Hortobágy plains and in the Kiskunság, but these territories have been reduced and are on the verge of disappearing.

Limonium gmelinii subsp. hungaricum
This plant appears on the Great Plain at the very end of summer. At first, only the occasional plant can be seen, but then suddenly, whole areas explode into purple bloom. It is not protected and many people pick it as a momento of their visit.

The plain is here coloured by ***Grasswort***
salicornia europaea

The early Hungarians bred this grey variety of cattle and for centuries it was the prevalent type here. It is well adapted to living in the extreme conditions of the Puszta, and in the Middle Ages, was highly sort after all over Europe. It is now being slowly reintroduced.

The long haired Hungarian racka is one of the most ancient and attractive of the world's sheep

The Hungarians were traditionally horsebreeders, and the Nóniusz variety was bred and trained at Hortobágy.

Autumn on the Puszta – spiders' webs are illuminated as dew drops catch the early morning light.

A sweep-well, in the frost

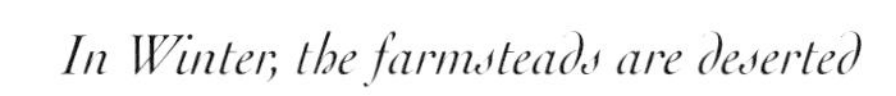

In Winter, the farmsteads are deserted

Acknowledgements

The photographer would like to thank first the publisher and designer.
Special thanks go to the colleagues of the National Parks for their help.
Separate thanks go to all those who supported the preparation of each photo.
The greatest thanks of all though, go to my family, who had to cope with my long absences.

The Books Supporters

The Government Office of the Hungarian Millenium, Budapest

Authority for Nature Conservation, Ministry of Environment

Books consulted:
István Capody: Our Protected Plants
Ottó Hermann: On the Use and Abuse of Birds.

Published by Officina '96 Kiadó
1088 Budapest, Szentkirályi u. 34
Tel: (36-1) 266-64-83, (36-1) 267-07-12, Fax: (36-1) 317-76-60
E-mail: officina@elender.hu
Responsible Publisher: Katalin Balogh
Design: Vera Köböl
Photosetting: Winter Fair Repro Studio, Szeged
Printing: Kossuth Nyomda Rt. Budapest

ISBN 963 9026 48 4